MAPS and MAPPING

HABITATS

By Susan Hoe

Science and curriculum consultant:
Debra Voege, M.A., science curriculum resource teacher

Gareth Stevens
Publishing

Please visit our web site at www.garethstevens.com.
For a free catalog describing our list of high-quality books, call 1-800-542-2595 (USA) or 1-800-387-3178 (Canada).
Our fax: 1-877-542-2596

Library of Congress Cataloging-in-Publication Data available upon request from publisher.

ISBN-10: 0-8368-9205-4   ISBN-13: 978-0-8368-9205-5 (lib. bdg.)
ISBN-10: 0-8368-9332-8   ISBN-13: 978-0-8368-9332-8 (softcover)

This edition first published in 2009 by
Gareth Stevens Publishing
A Weekly Reader® Company
1 Reader's Digest Road
Pleasantville, NY 10570-7000 USA

Gareth Stevens Senior Managing Editor: Lisa M. Herrington
Gareth Stevens Creative Director: Lisa Donovan
Gareth Stevens Art Director: Ken Crossland
Gareth Stevens Associate Editor: Amanda Hudson

Picture credits (t=top; b=bottom; c=center; l=left; r=right):
age fotostock/SuperStock: 13t; getmapping PLC: 24tc; Mike Hill/Alamy: 14b; Imagebroker/Alamy: 18c, 30b; iStock: 2, 10cr, 13b, 17c, 17b, 22t, 25b; Jupiter Images: 7b; www.mapart.co.uk: 7t, 12, 14c, 16c, 20c, 22b, 23, 26, 31tr; Ulli Seer/Getty Images: 5t. Shutterstock: 4bl, 6b, 8, 11, 16b, 17t, 20bl, 20br, 24tl, 24b, 25t, 25c, 27 all; Justin Spain: 4br, 9, 19b; Doug Steley/Alamy: 19t; Hayley Terry: 5b, 10bl, 21, 28, 29; ticktock Media Archive: 15; TongRo Image Stock/Fotosearch: 4t; Dave Watts/Alamy: 18bl, 18br.

Contents

Words in **bold** are defined in the glossary.

What Is a Map?

A **map** is a special drawing. This kind of drawing shows parts of an area. The area is drawn as if seen from above.

A map can show an area as big as the world. Or the area can be as small as a single garden!

Making a Map of an Island

Map Key

 Trees/woods

 Roads/footpaths

 Gray-roofed building

 Red-roofed building

 Pier

 Garden

Maps help us see things as if we were directly above them.

In this book, we will see how maps show us **habitats**. We will see where animals and plants make their homes.

Find the garden on the map.

Now look for the garden in the photo.

Why Do We Need Maps?

Maps help us find our way around. They give us all kinds of information about where we live!

A map can help you get from one place to another. It can show you where you are. It can show you where to go and how to get there.

Weather Map of the United States

This map shows what the weather will be like where you live.

What kinds of weather is this map showing?

Map of the World

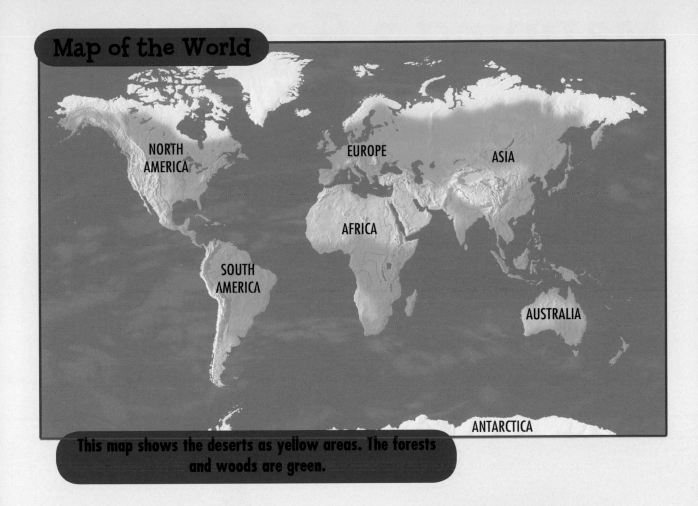

NORTH
AMERICA

EUROPE

ASIA

AFRICA

SOUTH
AMERICA

AUSTRALIA

ANTARCTICA

This map shows the deserts as yellow areas. The forests and woods are green.

Maps teach us important facts about places. We can learn about places close to home or on the other side of the world.

Maps can show whether land is flat or has hills. They can show where people and animals live. We can also learn what crops are grown. We can see what sorts of things are made in a place.

Maps are handy and easy to use. They can show us huge areas in a small amount of space. We can take them just about anywhere!

Mapping a Garden

Maps show a place as if you were looking down on it. That place can be your country or your town. It can even be a garden! A garden is one kind of habitat where animals and plants live.

A 3-D garden

The garden is a **three-dimensional (3-D)** space. All of the things in it are solid. They have length, width, and **depth**.

A 2-D Map

A map is a flat, or **two dimensional (2-D)**, drawing of a space. On a map, all of the objects in the garden look flat. They have only length and width.

To create a map, all the flat shapes are drawn on a piece of paper.

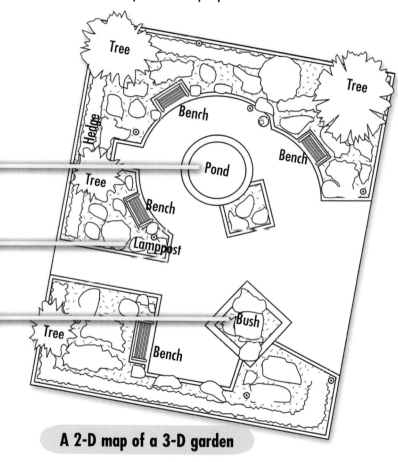

Tree

Tree

Hedge

Bench

Bench

Pond

Tree

Bench

Lamppost

Bush

Tree

Bench

A 2-D map of a 3-D garden

This map shows you how to find everything in the garden.

Can you find the pond in the photograph and on the map?

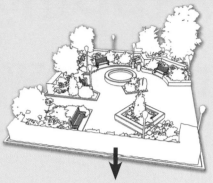

This drawing of the garden was made from photos.

Pretend you are able to float above the garden. Imagine looking down on it.

To create the 2-D map, draw all of the garden shapes that you see from above. Make the flat shapes on a piece of paper.

Mapping Habitats in a Town

Habitats are everywhere. Try to spot different habitats around your town.

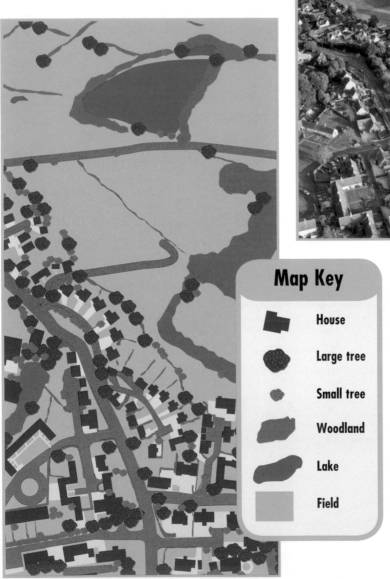

Map Key

	House
	Large tree
	Small tree
	Woodland
	Lake
	Field

The map (left) shows some of the habitats found in the town above. The map uses **symbols** to stand for each place. The map has a key. This **map key** is also called a legend. It tells you what each symbol means.

What are two different habitats found in the town?

Ecosystems

Many animals live in a habitat with plants and **microbes**. Microbes are tiny living things so small you cannot even see them.

Together, plants, animals, and microbes form a community called an **ecosystem**. They need one another to live.

This drawing shows an ecosystem in a woodland habitat. If there is a change to any one part, the other parts can be affected.

Woodland Ecosystem

The bird eats insects and fallen tree seeds.

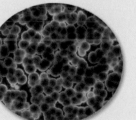

Insects eat the rotted leaves.

The bird drops the seeds.

More trees grow from the seeds.

Microbes break down the leaves and make them rot.

The trees drop their leaves.

Mapping Habitats in My Country

There are many habitats in the United States. Each has its own kind of land and weather. Each has its own plants and animals. Look at some of the habitats shown on this map of the United States. Use the map key to see the habitat in each area.

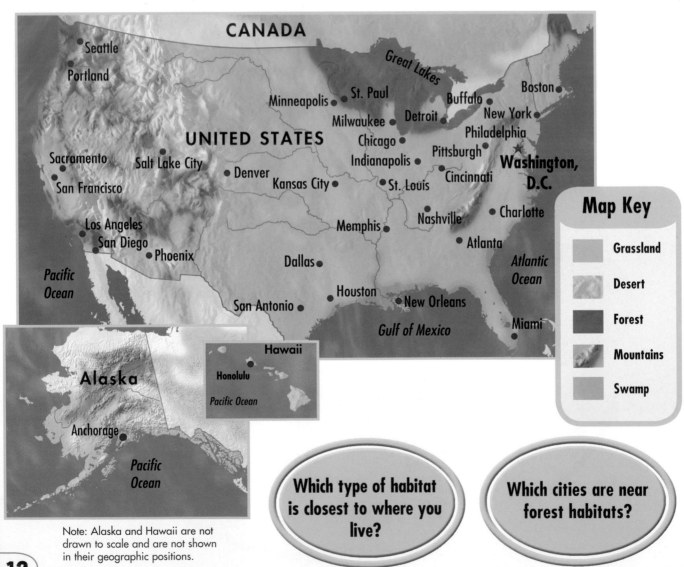

CANADA

Seattle
Portland

Great Lakes

Minneapolis • • St. Paul
Milwaukee • Detroit
Chicago •
Indianapolis •
Pittsburgh

Buffalo
New York •
Philadelphia

Boston •

UNITED STATES

Sacramento
San Francisco

Salt Lake City

Denver •
Kansas City •

St. Louis •

Cincinnati

Washington,
D.C.

Los Angeles
San Diego
• Phoenix

Memphis •

Nashville •
Atlanta •

• Charlotte

Dallas •

Pacific
Ocean

Houston •

San Antonio •

New Orleans •

Gulf of Mexico

Miami •

Atlantic
Ocean

Map Key

	Grassland
	Desert
	Forest
	Mountains
	Swamp

Hawaii

Alaska

Honolulu
Pacific Ocean

Anchorage

Pacific
Ocean

Note: Alaska and Hawaii are not drawn to scale and are not shown in their geographic positions.

Which type of habitat is closest to where you live?

Which cities are near forest habitats?

Wilderness Habitats

Some habitats are found in city or town parks. One such habitat might be a river or a stream. Even the soil beneath a rock can be a habitat. All kinds of plants and insects can live there. Other habitats contain even more kinds of wildlife. Many of these **wilderness** habitats are protected areas. The **government** makes sure that people do not harm plants and animals living in these areas.

The Volcanoes National Park is a rocky habitat. It is in Hawaii. This habitat is made up of black rocks from **volcanoes**. You can see ferns growing from the rocky land.

In Volcanoes National Park there are many colorful birds, such as this i'iwi. These birds need the plant life that grows in this habitat.

Mapping World Habitats

Maps of the world show that Earth has large areas of land called continents. There are seven continents in the world: North America, South America, Africa, Europe, Asia, Australia, and Antarctica. You can find many habitats on each of them. There are also habitats in the open waters around the continents.

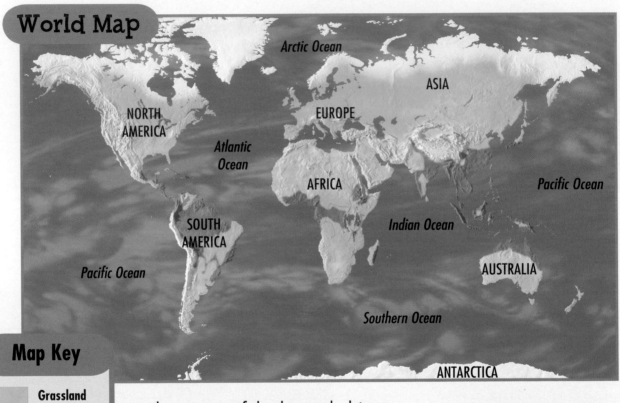

World Map

Arctic Ocean

ASIA

EUROPE

NORTH AMERICA

Atlantic Ocean

AFRICA

Pacific Ocean

Indian Ocean

SOUTH AMERICA

Pacific Ocean

AUSTRALIA

Southern Ocean

ANTARCTICA

Map Key

- Grassland
- Desert
- Rain forest
- Mountains
- Semi-desert
- Snow and ice

Look at some of the larger habitats found in the world. The map key tells you the kind of land in each habitat.

Find a desert habitat in Africa.

This jerboa lives in deserts in China and Mongolia. It does not need to drink water at all.

Map of North America

Most continents are divided into countries. Large oceans and seas surround the continents. The United States is on the continent of North America.

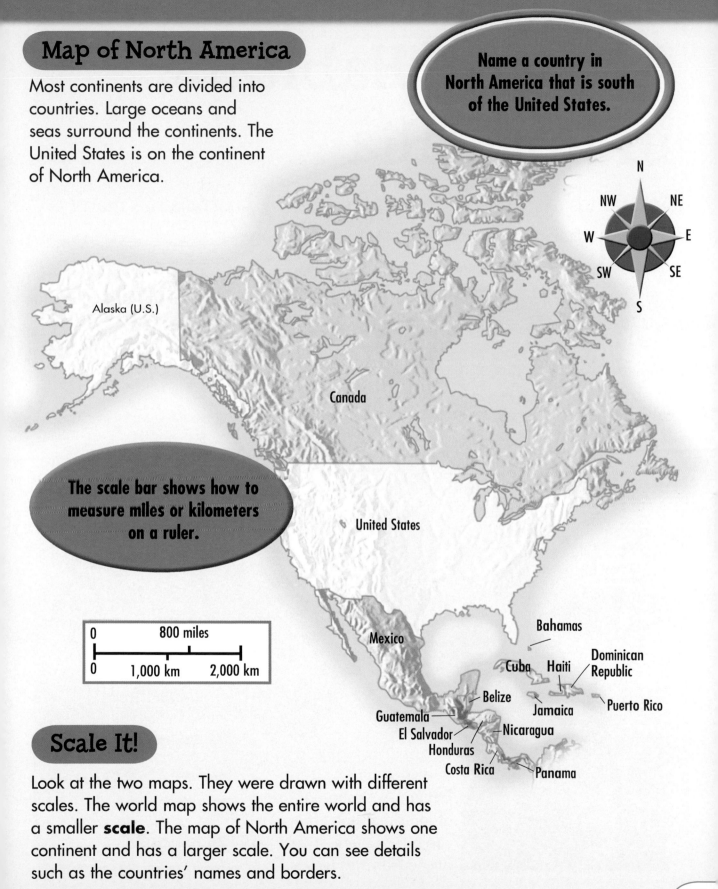

Name a country in North America that is south of the United States.

N
NW   NE
W   E
SW   SE
S

Alaska (U.S.)

Canada

The scale bar shows how to measure miles or kilometers on a ruler.

United States

0	800 miles	
0	1,000 km	2,000 km

Mexico

Bahamas

Cuba   Haiti

Dominican Republic

Belize

Puerto Rico

Guatemala

Jamaica

El Salvador   Nicaragua

Honduras

Costa Rica   Panama

Scale It!

Look at the two maps. They were drawn with different scales. The world map shows the entire world and has a smaller **scale**. The map of North America shows one continent and has a larger scale. You can see details such as the countries' names and borders.

A Map of Habitats in Australia

Australia is a continent. It is also a country. Australia has many different habitats.

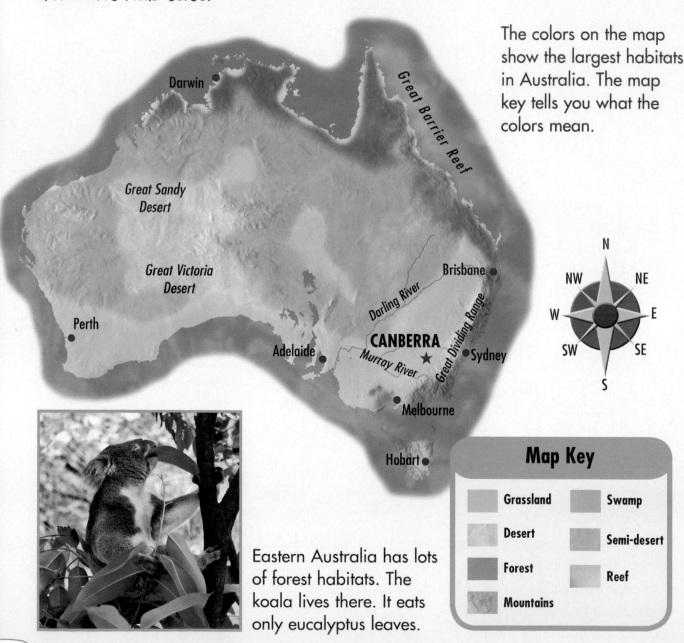

The colors on the map show the largest habitats in Australia. The map key tells you what the colors mean.

Eastern Australia has lots of forest habitats. The koala lives there. It eats only eucalyptus leaves.

Map Key

	Grassland		Swamp
	Desert		Semi-desert
	Forest		Reef
	Mountains		

Much of Australia has desert and semi-desert habitats. Often, the desert is called the Outback.

Ayers Rock is a huge rock formation in the Outback. It is in the region of Australia known as the Northern **Territory**. Its watering holes and rock caves attract many desert animals.

The red kangaroo is one of many animals that live in the desert.

The Great Barrier Reef

The Great Barrier Reef is an underwater habitat in Australia. Many fish and other sea creatures live among the coral reefs.

The hard coral reef is made from the skeletons of sea animals. There are many types of coral. Some are flat. Some look like lace. Some even look like a human brain!

Mapping a Watering Hole in Australia

A watering hole is a sunken area of land that fills with water. In Australia's Outback, a watering hole can be a habitat for desert animals. They gather there to drink and cool off. A watering hole can be natural or made by people.

In Australia, natural watering holes like this one attract different desert animals.

The dingo, a type of wild Australian dog, can live in many different habitats.

Red kangaroos can go for a long time without water. They get it by eating plants.

This watering hole was made by people. It is part of a very large cattle ranch, also called a cattle station. The watering hole has a high rim that holds the water in place.

There is little rainfall in this habitat. The only plants are dry bushes. At this watering hole, there is a small fenced area. This area is used for rounding up, or mustering, the cattle.

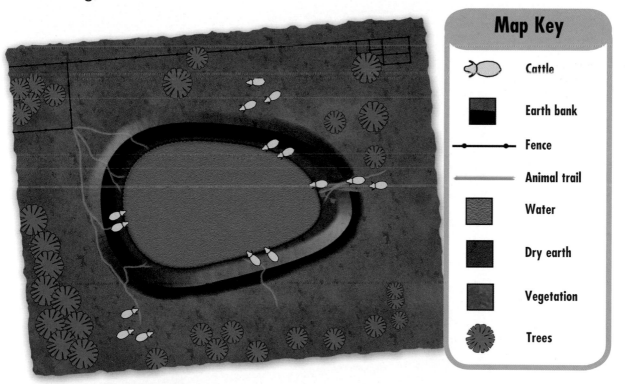

Map Key

🐄	Cattle
⬛	Earth bank
●─●─●	Fence
▬	Animal trail
⬛	Water
⬛	Dry earth
⬛	Vegetation
✺	Trees

The map of this watering hole uses symbols. They stand for the different animals, objects, and **land features**. The map key helps you understand what the different symbols mean.

More Map Information

This map uses color to show temperatures around the world in the month of January. The map key colors show the highest and lowest temperatures. What is the temperature range where you live?

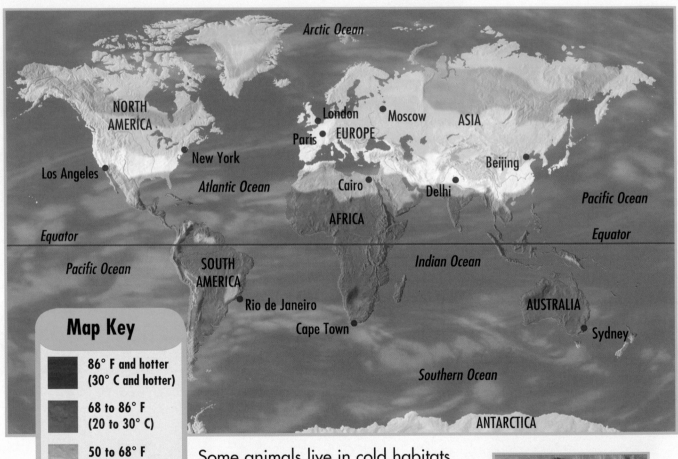

Arctic Ocean

NORTH AMERICA

London
Moscow
ASIA
Paris
EUROPE

New York

Los Angeles

Atlantic Ocean

Beijing

Cairo

Delhi

Pacific Ocean

AFRICA

Equator

Equator

Pacific Ocean

SOUTH AMERICA

Indian Ocean

AUSTRALIA

Rio de Janeiro

Cape Town

Sydney

Southern Ocean

ANTARCTICA

Map Key

■	86° F and hotter (30° C and hotter)
■	68 to 86° F (20 to 30° C)
■	50 to 68° F (10 to 20° C)
□	32 to 50° F (0 to 10° C)
■	-4 to 32° F (-20 to 0° C)
■	-22 to -4° F (-30 to -20° C)
■	-22° F and colder (-30° C and colder)

Some animals live in cold habitats. Others live in warmer habitats.

The polar bear lives in icy regions.

The lion roams warm grasslands.

Using a Map Grid

A **grid** is a mapping tool. It helps you find a specific place on a map. A grid is made of lines that form squares.

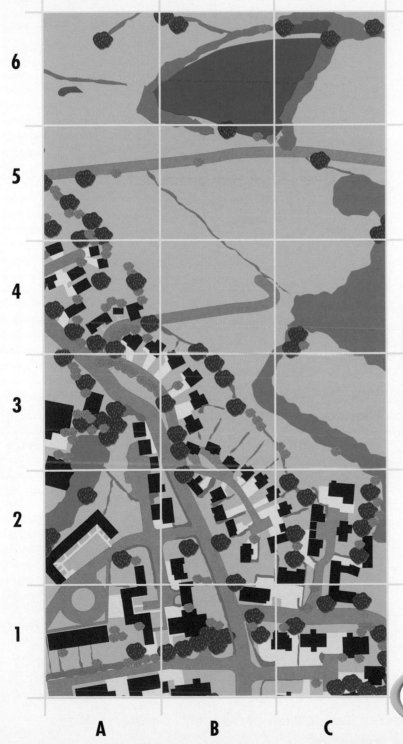

The squares on this map go left to right to make rows. Each row has a number. The squares also go from bottom to top to make columns. Each column has a letter.

Each square can be named by both a letter and a number. Together, the letter and number are called **coordinates**.

Map Key

🏠	House	🌲	Woodland
🌳	Large tree	🪱	Lake
🌿	Small tree	⬜	Field

To find the lake habitat, check the map key. Its coordinates are B6. Put your finger on B. Move your finger up column B until you find row 6. The lake is there!

Give the coordinates of the largest woodland area.

Measuring for Maps

Before you can draw a map, you must figure out the size and shape of the area. This means figuring out how to measure large areas.

This man uses special equipment to measure distances between points.

Mapmakers use their measurements to draw their maps. The maps on these pages show an amusement park.

Scale: Shrinking to Fit

Mapmakers gather all their measurements. Then they figure out how to fit them onto a piece of paper. So they shrink, or **scale** down, the real measurements to make a map.

0	50 feet
	15 meters

This map shows a fairly large area. It uses a scale of 50 feet (15 meters). Many
objects can be seen, but they are quite small.

Different scales can be used to map the same area. A different scale can change what you see. Some maps show large areas on a sheet of paper. Other maps show smaller areas, so the same objects look bigger and have more features.

The map scale is like a ruler. It shows the connection between distance on the map and distance on the ground. This way you can figure out real distances on the map.

0	25 feet
	8 meters

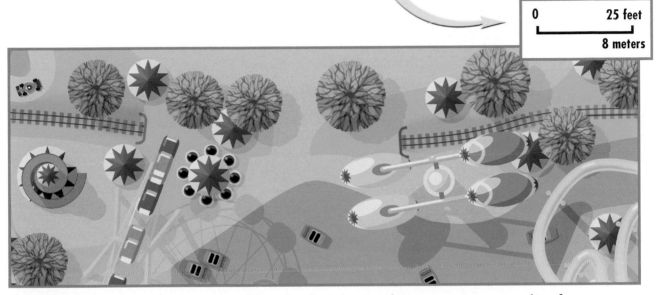

This map shows a smaller area than the first map. This map uses a scale of 25 feet (8 m). You see fewer objects on this map, but they seem closer.

0	15 feet
	5 meters

This map has the largest scale. It shows an even smaller area. You see fewer objects, but they seem even closer.

Mapping With Computers

Many years ago, people had to travel to figure out the shape of the land. Today, mapmakers use computer equipment.

Mapmakers can take many photographs of the ground from an airplane.

This photograph shows the ground as seen from the airplane.

Pictures and measurements are taken from an airplane and sent to computers. The computers use the pictures to draw maps.

Satellites also take pictures of Earth from space.

A satellite circling Earth

Pictures are taken from space, too. The pictures are sent back to Earth. They are put together to make full pictures of our planet, like the one shown here. These pictures can then be turned into maps.

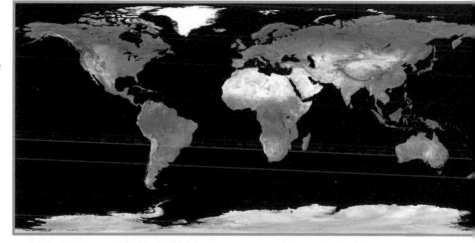

Changing Maps

Satellites can produce road maps that help you find your way. These maps change as you move. The maps are called **GPS (Global Positioning System)** maps.

A GPS map at work in a car

Using a Grid to Map Animal Habitats

Australia has many unusual animals. Some of the animals are not found anywhere else in the world. They live in different habitats in Australia. Use your map skills to put Australia's animals in their correct habitats!

Map Key

- Grassland
- Desert
- Rain forest
- Swamp
- Semi-desert
- Reef

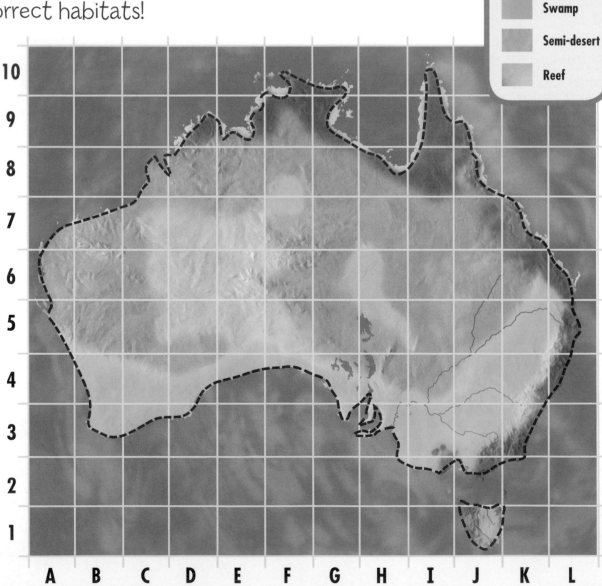

How to Make a Map of the Animals of Australia

1. Copy the map of Australia on page 26 onto a blank sheet of paper. Color your map to show the different habitats.

2. Now make a map key. Draw pictures of the animals below. Write the names of the animals.

3. See the letters and numbers beneath the pictures. Use them to find each animal's coordinates on the map grid. (You can read about grids and coordinates on page 21.)

4. Follow the coordinates for each animal. Draw the animals in their correct spots on the map.

5. Some of the animals live in more than one habitat. Which habitat seems best suited to each animal on your map?

Animal Map Key

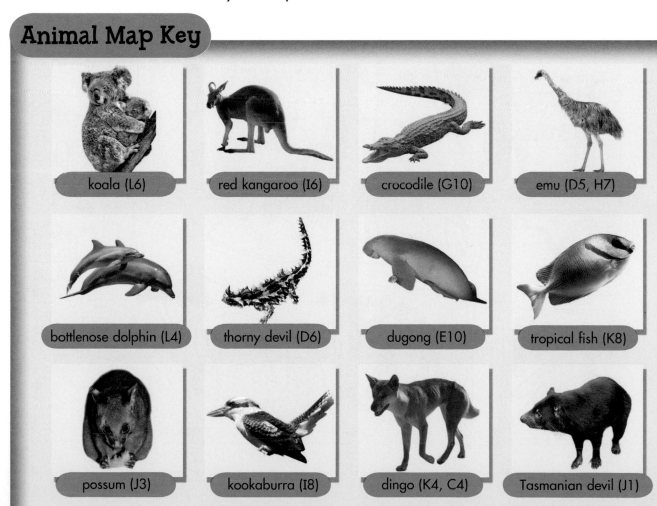

koala (L6)

red kangaroo (I6)

crocodile (G10)

emu (D5, H7)

bottlenose dolphin (L4)

thorny devil (D6)

dugong (E10)

tropical fish (K8)

possum (J3)

kookaburra (I8)

dingo (K4, C4)

Tasmanian devil (J1)

Making a Map of a Habitat Zoo

Have you ever been on a trip to the zoo? Why not make a map of your own zoo, filled with different kinds of habitats? Make sure you place your animals into their natural habitats.

What shape is your zoo?

Does your zoo have a snack bar? Does it have restrooms, picnic tables, or water fountains?

William's Wonderful Zoo

Step 1

Draw the shape of your zoo on a piece of paper.

Step 2

Decide which habitats you want in your zoo. Decide where to put them. Map out a trail your friends can follow when visiting your zoo. Put in water fountains, trash cans, and other helpful items.

Step 3

Draw the animals you have chosen. Pick your favorite animals, and be sure to place them in their correct habitats! Color the animals and habitats.

Give your zoo a name.

Map Key

Step 4

Make your map key using the symbols, colors, and designs on your map.

Desert	Tigers	Elephants	Ticket office	Footpath
Water	Snakes	Giraffes	Gift shop	Snack bar
Forest	Parrots	Meerkats	Restroom	Eating area
Grassland	Monkeys	Camels	Trash can	First aid
Rain forest	Polar bears	Turtles	Water fountain	Fence
Arctic	Walruses	Tropical fish		Barrier

Glossary

coordinates: a pair of numbers and letters used to locate a place on a map

depth: the length from the top of a space or an object to the bottom

ecosystem: a community of living things

government: a group of people who make the laws and rule in a country or an area

GPS (Global Positioning System): an instrument that shows how to get to a place. In a moving car, the instrument shows the driver directions on a screen.

grid: a pattern of lines, usually going both up and down and across, used as a way of finding locations on a map. Grids are often used with coordinates.

habitats: areas or environments where plants or animals are most likely to be found. Most habitats are suited to certain kinds of life, such as fish (in a water habitat) or tropical plants (in a rain forest habitat).

land features: natural areas found on Earth. Mountains, rivers, forests, and deserts are all land features.

map: a picture or chart showing features of an area

map key: the space on a map that shows the meaning of any pictures or colors on the map

microbes: tiny living things so small they cannot be seen without a microscope

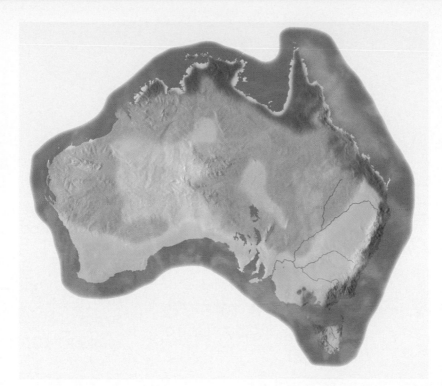

satellites: objects sent into space that circle and study Earth or other bodies in space. They then send information back to Earth.

scale: the amount by which the measurement of an area is shrunk to fit on a map. The map scale is a drawing or symbol that tells how to measure distances on a map.

symbols: pictures or drawings that stand for different things

territory: area of land and water that belongs to a single country. Maps show borders of territories.

three-dimensional (3-D): appearing as a solid thing that has length, width, and depth

two-dimensional (2-D): appearing as a flat shape with only length and width

volcanoes: openings in Earth's surface that throw off hot lava, ash, and gases from deep in Earth

wilderness: an area in which very few people live and that is mostly left in its natural state

Index